SKINNYTINIS

ALL THE FUN FOR HALF THE CALORIES

A Recipe Book
That Shows Social
Drinkers How to Enjoy
Their Martinis
and Stay Skinny!

TERESA MARIE HOWES

PHOTOGRAPHS BY JASON WYCHE

 JOHN WILEY & SONS, INC.

For general information on our other products and services or for technical support, please
contact our Customer Care Department within the United States at (800) 762-2974, outside
the United States at (317) 572-3993 or fax (317) 572-4002.

Wiley also publishes its books in a variety of electronic formats. Some content that appears
in print may not be available in electronic books. For more information about Wiley products, visit our web site at www.wiley.com.

Credits: The glasses in the following photographs are courtesy of MOLO (FLOAT series),
molodesign.com: Skinny Mojito (page 83), Skinny Madras (page 77), and Skinny Mudslide
(page 84). The glass in the following photograph is courtesy of Calvin Klein Glassware,
calvinklein.com: Cactus Chill (page 69). The glass in the following photograph is courtesy of
Alessi Glassware, alessi.com: Skinny Piña Colada (page 87).

Food styling by Jamie Kimm
Prop styling by Leslie Siegel

Library of Congress Cataloging-in-Publication Data:
Howes, Teresa Marie.
SkinnyTinis : all the fun for half the calories / Teresa Marie Howes.
p. cm.
Includes index.
ISBN 978-0-470-44706-2 (cloth : alk. paper)
1. Cocktails. 2. Low-calorie diet--Recipes. I. Title. II. Title: Skinny tinis.
TX951.H688 2009
641.8'74--dc22
2008041813
Printed in China

10 9 8 7 6 5 4 3 2 1

FOR MY FRIEND SHARON,
who always cherished a fine chocolate martini.
We miss her dearly.

CONTENTS

6 INTRODUCTION

12 GETTING YOUR SKINNY BAR READY

16 DRINKS, DRINKS, AND MORE DRINKS!

99 LOVE THE RECIPES... BUT WHAT DO I DO WHEN I'M OUT?

132 THE SKINNY TRICKS

143 INDEX

INTRODUCTION

After drinking socially for over ten years, I have come to realize that cocktails and my life are not going to part ways anytime soon. I am a social drinker, honest and true! Mimosas during brunch with my family, a mojito on a sunny afternoon with the ladies, and the occasional cocktail before dinner with my honey are things that I do not want to relinquish. My primary interest now, as a woman over thirty, is how to manage this part of my social life without continuing to add pounds to my frame!

With a background in nutrition and a career in the weight-loss industry, I've certainly always "known" what was good for me. Now I have reached an age where I'm being forced to act on it. Gone are the days when I could simply think about losing five pounds and see them gone the following week. At this point, the proverbial battle over five to ten pounds has become World War III. For me, it takes a serious fight to see the scale drop, and I'd like to think I'm not alone.

So how do we do this? How do we maintain or lose weight without giving up small pleasures in life like a night out on the town with the girls or a stiff martini after a long day at the office? That was the question that prompted me to begin looking at alcohol differently. Instead of trying to avoid it, I'd prefer to find ways to modify recipes and habits so I can still enjoy my favorites, but with fewer toxic effects. Hence the advent of SkinnyTinis! I was so proud of my concoctions and revelations that I felt compelled to share them with the rest of the social drinkers who share my struggle.

The recipes in this book have been tested, and users have rated them just as tasty as their high-calorie counterparts (if not tastier). They were created using easy-to-find low-sugar mixers, high-quality alcohol, and clever garnishes, much like those you would find in a sleek martini bar in Manhattan. The only difference? They have less than half the calories! Bonus chapters in this book offer advice on trimly navigating the overwhelming cocktail menus found in most restaurants and bars, hints on how to burn off the cocktails you've enjoyed, plus a few other fine tips and tricks I've learned from life experience, research, and my fantastic skinny girlfriends.

HOW DO SKINNYTINIS WORK?

Some of the SkinnyTini recipes are completely original and were designed to be refreshing, intoxicating, and low calorie! Others should be very familiar to you, as they have been served since the days of the speakeasy. These common recipes have simply been remixed using new, innovative reduced-calorie or sugar-free products.

Martinis served in a bar or restaurant will typically contain over 300 calories. This is due mostly to the combination of various high-calorie, high-sugar alcohols and liqueurs. Since a martini is known for its powerful alcohol content, the true challenge in creating SkinnyTinis was to find a way to maintain alcohol potency and portion size while eliminating excess calories.

There are two key tricks that make SkinnyTinis possible: a) taking "alcohol-calorie efficiency" to the extreme and b) taking advantage of all the low-sugar and sugar-free products currently on the market. To understand what I mean by alcohol-calorie efficiency, look at the chart on page 8, which shows how many calories different types of alcohol contain, relative to their alcohol potency. Then check the chart on page 9 to see how quickly the calories from nonalcoholic mixers can add up. These charts make it very easy to understand how a standard martini can contain up to 400 calories with relatively little alcohol potency.

All SkinnyTinis use only distilled spirits (vodka, rum, tequila, whisky, or gin), which have only 64 calories per ounce but offer 40 percent alcohol potency. Note that total alcohol content and exact calories per ounce vary by brand, so you might want to do a little research on your favorites to be sure they fall in this calorie range. The alcohol calories constitute about 90 percent of the total calories in each SkinnyTini recipe. You can rest assured that the thirty recipes in the SkinnyTini section of this book still pack a mighty punch, with at least two ounces of 70 to 80 proof distilled spirits and an average of only 140 calories!

In addition to the thirty SkinnyTinis, you'll also find recipes for twenty Skinny Cocktails. These drinks contain slightly less alcohol and roughly 20 percent fewer calories than Skinny-Tinis and are, for the most part, remakes of familiar cocktails. They should be served over ice in highball or other cocktail glasses. In these recipes, the high-calorie alcohols and sugar-

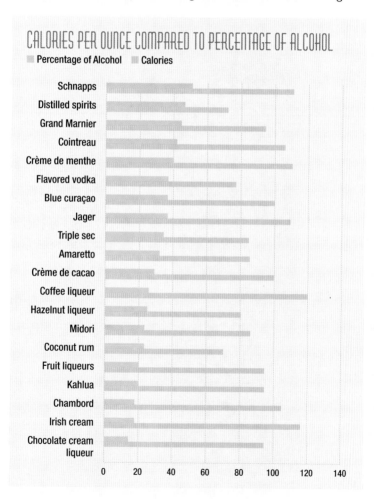

CALORIES PER OUNCE COMPARED TO PERCENTAGE OF ALCOHOL

Percentage of Alcohol   Calories

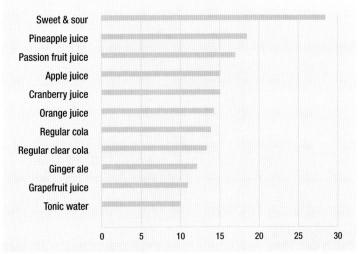

based mixers have been replaced with lighter options. As a result, the average Skinny Cocktail still has 1½ ounces of alcohol, the standard amount you would find in a cocktail ordered in a restaurant, yet only 117 calories! The last set of recipes in this book are drinks you could cleverly order while out on the town. To date, they are not quite popular enough to order by name, but a little instruction and a smile for the bartender will ensure you receive a Skinny Cocktail with an average of only 111 calories!

In this recipe book, all original Skinny recipes will list the total calories for a 5-ounce drink. A Skinny recipe that is a remake of an original will list both the calories in the Skinny recipe and the original recipe, so you'll see just how simple it can be to save up to 300 calories by making a few minor modifications.

This book will not only allow you to enjoy alcohol in moderation with fewer calories, but also to impress your friends at your next dinner party or social event. What could be more delicious than serving a glamorous, original SkinnyTini and saving your guests hundreds of calories?

A WORD ABOUT SUGAR-FREE PRODUCTS

Low-sugar and sugar-free mixes can significantly lower calories while maintaining flavor and are a vital component of SkinnyTinis. Artificial sweeteners are part of our culture, and their consumption has nearly doubled in the past ten years. You can find them in pink, yellow, or blue packets, in bottles, and in sugar-free products of all kinds. Many SkinnyTini ingredients do contain an artificial sweetener. They were selected because they are readily available and easy to find.

There is no research to support claims that artificial sweeteners are in any way detrimental to one's health. In fact, many health professionals stress the benefits of low-calorie sweeteners, especially for overweight individuals and those with diabetes. And unlike sugar, they do not promote dental cavities.

Still, many consumers may prefer the natural route. The good news is that if you want to avoid artificial sweeteners for any reason, you can still enjoy SkinnyTinis! Recently, more natural low-calorie sugar substitutes have become available. The herb stevia (*Stevia rebaudiana*) is 200 to 300 times sweeter than sugar and is available in liquid form online and in the supplement section of most health food stores. Also available is a substance known as Erythritol, which is about 70 percent as sweet as sugar. You can find it in crystal form under several brand names, including Organic Zero and Zsweet, at most health food stores and online.

GIVING YOUR SKINNYTINI A NATURAL KICK

When a SkinnyTini recipe calls for liquid Sweet'N Low, try using stevia instead. Just 2 drops of SteviaClear is as sweet as 1 teaspoon of sugar or 10 drops of Sweet'N Low. SteviaClear also comes in twelve flavors, including Valencia orange, vanilla cream, and lemon drop. Erythritol does not dissolve as well in liquid, but the martini shaking sure helps! SkinnyTini recipes also use low-sugar juices and diet sodas. If you prefer to avoid these, simply use the full-sugar versions, but dilute them with

club soda or water to avoid increasing calories. If you feel these changes alter the flavor of the recipe too much, don't bother, but expect a 25 to 30 percent increase in calories per drink. Many recipes also call for a sugar-free flavored syrup such as peach, coconut, mango, vanilla, or caramel. Eliminating these will have a larger impact on the flavor of the drink, as well as the calorie count, but it certainly can be done! Try using natural nectars, but expect them to have roughly 20 calories per ounce, and be sure to calculate that into your daily calorie count if you keep one.

GETTING YOUR SKINNY BAR READY

Over fifty different ingredients are used in this book. Some are uncommon and only used once or twice. Once you select your favorite recipes, you'll have to make sure you have those special ingredients on hand. There are also a few very basic ingredients that you'll want to make sure you have, as you never know when you'll need to shake up a SkinnyTini, kick off your heels, and relax! Use the lists at right on your next shopping trip to make sure you have the basics stocked and your fridge is ready to go when you are.

Having all these ingredients on hand ensures you'll be able to make nearly thirty of the recipes in this book. The first column alone makes up thirteen different Skinny recipes! You'll be amazed and your friends will be impressed with how easy it is to make these small changes that add up to big calorie savings.

SHOPPING TIPS

• Be sure to select "low pulp" or "pulp-free" orange juice; even then, you might want to strain the entire carton of juice

NEVER RUN OUT OF THESE

- Vodka
- Light orange juice
- Lime juice
- Vanilla vodka
- Light cranberry juice
- Liquid Sweet'N Low
- Lemon juice
- Light ruby red grapefruit juice
- Sugar-free peach syrup
- White rum
- Low-fat milk (2%)
- Citrus vodka
- Pineapple juice

THESE ADD FLAIR

- Club soda
- Diet ginger ale
- White tequila
- Coffee
- Fat-free hot cocoa mix
- Gin
- Grapefruit juice
- Sugar-free vanilla coffee creamer
- Sugar-free coconut syrup
- Diet lemon-lime soda
- Red wine
- Sugar-free mango syrup
- Fresh mint sprigs

before pouring it in the martini shaker. Same goes for fresh lemon or lime juices, as pulp does not add much to the aesthetic appeal of a martini.

- Flavored vodkas can vary in alcohol and calorie content. For example, citron/citrus vodkas can range from 56 to 100 calories and 35 to 40 percent alcohol per ounce.

- Be careful when purchasing cranberry juice for Skinny recipes. "Diet" cranberry has only 5 calories per 8-ounce serving, but it comes with a very "diety" flavor. If you are not accustomed to it, be sure to select "light," with just 3 more calories per ounce and significantly less "fake-sugar" taste.

- You can find Sweet'N Low in the coffee aisle of any grocery store, near the packets of various powdered sweeteners. You may also find a liquid version if you prefer that product. If you opt for that, be sure to modify the quantities, as the level of sweetness varies.

- Flavored sugar-free syrups can sometimes be found in the coffee aisle of high-end grocery and specialty stores such as World Market. Alternatively, over twenty-seven flavors can be found at www.torani.com.

- Be watchful when you are shopping for vanilla coffee creamer. There is a difference in the flavor and calorie count between sugar-free and fat-free variations. Most recipes use sugar-free, as it has just 30 calories per ounce; the fat-free version has 50.

- Calorie-free sweetened waters can be found in the water aisle at most grocery stores, and flavored sparkling waters are typically in the alcohol mixer section near the club soda and tonic water.

THE SKINNYTINIS WEBSITE

If you have a favorite flavor combination or a signature cocktail and you're curious as to how many calories it has, don't forget to visit the SkinnyTinis website at www.skinnytinis.com. It is a comprehensive site that will allow you to custom design your very own personal SkinnyTini! Your recipe will come complete with an adorable recipe card and total calories. You can e-mail your recipe to your friends, or simply print it and hand out the copies as favors at your next cocktail party. If it's a really great recipe, it may even get added to the universal database and be SkinnyTini Certified! In addition to creating your signature SkinnyTini, you can also learn more about how alcohol impacts your head, your heart, and your figure. You can even become a "Certified SkinnyTini Mixologist" if you pass the short quiz. You'll always find a ton of updated, fun information on www.skinnytins.com, so you'll never run out of inspiration or support when it comes to managing your fantastic social life and your waistlines!

DRINKS, DRINKS, AND MORE DRINKS!

SKINNYTINI RECIPES

REMINDER: Most SkinnyTini recipes contain 2 ounces of 80-proof alcohol (vodka, rum, tequila, whisky, or gin) and 3 ounces of low-calorie mixer and have on average only 140 calories!

ANTIGANTINI
140 CALORIES

2 ounces vodka
2½ ounce light cranberry juice
½ ounce sugar-free peach syrup

Add all ingredients to a cocktail shaker with ice and shake for 10 to 15 seconds. Strain into a 5-ounce martini glass, garnish with a peach wedge and serve.

SKINNY TIDBIT It was a holiday trip to Antigua (and the thought of a winter-toned body in a bikini) that posed the problem of how to have a fantastic vacation, enjoy a fun cocktail, and not feel bad about it while lying on the beach! This quandary is the root of the SkinnyTinis concept, and the recipes followed from there.

ALMOND BLISS
141 CALORIES

1 ounce hot water
1 tsp fat-free cocoa powder
2 ounces vanilla vodka
1 ounce low-fat milk (2%)
½ ounce sugar-free almond syrup
½ ounce sugar-free coconut syrup

Add hot water to a cocktail shaker and add cocoa powder. Stir well to ensure you have a fully mixed chocolate base. Be sure to stir rather than closing the shaker and shaking, as hot liquids can sometimes have an explosive effect. Add the remaining ingredients with ice, stir well to cool the mixture, then close the shaker and shake for 10 to 15 seconds. Strain into a 5-ounce martini glass.

PREPARATION TIDBIT If making more than one serving, prepare the hot cocoa mix according to the package directions and cool before mixing. Then simply add one ounce to the shaker per serving. This will save you some time and trouble while you are entertaining.

SKINNY TIDBIT The Almond Bliss SkinnyTini is almost as tasty as the famous Almond Joy candy bar but with about half the calories! This is an ultrasweet recipe, perfect to serve after dinner in lieu of a traditional plated desert. If you find it too sweet, use regular vodka instead of vanilla to curb the sugary flavor.

CARIBBEAN KILLER
147 CALORIES

2 ounces white rum
1½ ounces light ruby red grapefruit juice
1½ ounces light orange juice
½ tablet pink grapefruit Airborne*

Add the rum and juices to a cocktail shaker with ice, shake, and pour into a 5-ounce martini glass—then add the Airborne tablet. Serve the drink while the tablet is fizzing, and be patient, because it dissolves slowly.

SKINNY TIDBIT The original SkinnyTini, and not your everyday tropical cocktail! This unique martini gets its intrigue from the Airborne, which adds a fun, tasty, fizzy effect and has just 5 calories per tablet.

* Airborne is a brand name for a tablet that is popular for strengthening your immune system and recommended during travel. It can be found at drug stores in the OTC aisles.

THE BAY OF BENGAL
147 CALORIES

2 ounces vodka
2 ounces light cranberry juice
½ ounce sugar-free mango syrup
½ ounce mango nectar

Add all ingredients to a cocktail shaker with ice and shake for 10 to 15 seconds. Strain into a 5-ounce martini glass.

SKINNY TIDBIT Mangos originated in East India, Burma, and the Andaman Islands bordering the Bay of Bengal, and this sweet-and-sour combination is as intriguing as its namesake. If you prefer a tarter SkinnyTini, substitute lemon juice for the mango nectar and trade 5 calories for the extra-sour kick. For a sexy and original garnish, skewer diced fresh mangos and/or cranberries on a toothpick or dice and freeze mango and drop in the bottom of the glass.

CANDY APPLE MARTINI
147 CALORIES

1 ounce vodka
1 ounce apple vodka
3 ounces light apple juice
¼ ounce (splash) grenadine

Add all ingredients to a cocktail shaker with ice and shake for 10 to 15 seconds. Strain into a 5-ounce martini glass.

SKINNY TIDBIT As adorable and delicious as the name implies. This recipe is similar to the appletini, but comes with a beautiful red color thanks to the grenadine, which also adds a delightful candylike flavor. Grenadine is high in calories and contains no alcohol, but when used sparingly it can add charm to any cocktail. Be sure to garnish this SkinnyTini with skewered maraschino cherries.

CABO SUNSET
148 CALORIES

2 ounces vodka
1½ ounces light orange juice
1 ounce grapefruit juice
½ ounce sugar-free mango syrup

Add all ingredients to a cocktail shaker with ice and shake for 10 to 15 seconds. Strain into a 5-ounce martini glass.

SKINNY TIDBIT This SkinnyTini is a crowd-pleaser, thanks to its light, refreshing flavor combination of tangy grapefruit and sweet mango. You can also mix this drink with white wine in lieu of the vodka for a total calorie content of just 60 calories, or use peach vodka if you prefer a sweeter cocktail. Both these options give the Cabo Sunset a lighter feel, making it more appropriate for "sunrise" occasions like breakfast and brunch.

CARAMEL LATTE MARTINI
136 CALORIES

1½ ounces strongly brewed coffee
2 ounces vanilla vodka
1 ounce low-fat milk (2%)
½ ounce sugar-free caramel syrup

Be sure the coffee is cooled before adding it to the shaker with ice and the remaining ingredients. Remember, hot liquids can have an explosive effect when shaken in an airtight container. Strain into a 5-ounce martini glass.

SKINNY TIDBIT If your favorite coffeehouse could serve liquor, this would be their best seller! With the same ingredients as a caramel latte, plus vanilla vodka, this drink is sure to leave you satisfied and energized! Using 2% milk adds just 5 extra calories over nonfat and gives it a smoother, more fulfilling flavor.

COTTON CANDY
145 CALORIES

2 ounces vanilla vodka
2 ounces light ruby red grapefruit juice
1 ounce low-fat milk (2%)

Add all ingredients to a cocktail shaker with ice and shake for 10 to 15 seconds. Strain into a 5-ounce martini glass.

SKINNY TIDBIT The Cotton Candy came to fruition at a girls' night/ slumber party. The ultrapink, ultragirly combination of vanilla and sweet citrus makes this the perfect dessert-style cocktail to share with your fun, fabulous girlfriends. You can also blend this cocktail with ice for a fun "fluffy" effect.

CITRUS SPLASH
147 CALORIES

2 ounces vodka
1 ounce light orange juice
1 ounce light grapefruit juice
½ ounce fresh lime juice
½ ounce fresh lemon juice

Add all ingredients to a cocktail shaker with ice and shake for 10 to 15 seconds. Strain into a 5-ounce martini glass.

PREPARATION TIDBIT If you're serving a large group, whether it's this recipe or any SkinnyTini that has several nonalcoholic ingredients, save yourself some time and frustration by preparing pitchers of all the mixers ahead of time. When your guests arrive, you simply add 2 ounces of alcohol and 3 ounces of the mixer and shake. This still allows you to be the glamorous host, shaking and serving up martinis, yet gives you more time to spend with your guests throughout the evening.

SKINNY TIDBIT This cocktail packs over 30 milligrams of vitamin C—almost half the recommended daily intake—and with that comes a powerful citrus jolt.

COCONUT CLOUDS
144 CALORIES

2 ounces white rum
½ ounce low-fat milk (2%)
½ ounce sugar-free coconut syrup
½ ounce pineapple juice
½ cup ice for blending

Add all ingredients including ice to a blender. Mix on high speed for a minute, pour into a glass, garnish, and serve.

SKINNY TIDBIT This is a slightly more sophisticated spin on your traditional piña colada, and it gets its name from the fluffy texture of the blended ice. You can dress it up by garnishing it with a pineapple wedge and classic maraschino cherry.

CREAMSICLE
136 CALORIES

2 ounces vanilla vodka
2½ ounces light orange juice
½ ounce sugar-free peach syrup

Add all ingredients to a cocktail shaker with ice and shake for 10 to 15 seconds. Strain into a 5-ounce martini glass.

SKINNY TIDBIT A childhood favorite transformed into a sophisticated and delicious SkinnyTini that has just a few more calories than the famous ice cream bar itself! Enjoy this one for dessert on a warm summer day. Garnish with a Popsicle stick and orange slices.

FRUIT BASKETS
138 CALORIES

2 ounces fruit vodka, such as cherry, strawberry, peach, or
  watermelon
2½ ounces sugar-free fruit-flavored water
½ ounce sugar-free fruit-flavored syrup

Add all ingredients to a cocktail shaker with ice and shake for 10 to
15 seconds. Strain into a 5-ounce martini glass.

SKINNY TIDBIT Fruit baskets are wonderful, crisp, and easy to make.
Add elegance and variety with a garnish of fresh fruit, either skewered,
dropped loose into the drink, or draped over the edge of the glass.

THE GINGERSNAP
130 CALORIES

2 ounces gin
3 ounces diet ginger ale
¼ ounce (splash) of lime juice
Dash of nutmeg

Add all ingredients to a cocktail shaker with ice and shake for 10 to 15 seconds. Strain into a 5-ounce martini glass. Be careful as you shake any SkinnyTini containing a carbonated mixer, as it can have a powerful and slightly messy effect on your kitchen. To ease the situation, wrap the shaker in a towel and shake gently.

SKINNY TIDBIT This drink was designed to recall the familiar flavor of a spicy gingersnap cookie. The nutmeg adds aesthetic appeal because of the intriguing way it drifts throughout the SkinnyTini.

APPLE VINE
137 CALORIES

2 ounces apple vodka
1½ ounces light white grape juice
1½ ounces grape-flavored water

Add all ingredients to a cocktail shaker with ice and shake for 10 to 15 seconds. Strain into a 5-ounce martini glass.

SKINNY TIDBIT This drink is an example of accidental excellence. It was created after a bottle of light white grape juice was confused with apple juice and purchased by mistake. For a sweet take on the classic martini, skewer fresh grapes on a toothpick as if they were olives and drop them in the glass.

PINK PANTHER
127 CALORIES

2 ounces citrus vodka
1½ ounces light ruby red grapefruit juice
1½ ounces light cranberry juice

Add all ingredients to a cocktail shaker with ice and shake for 10 to 15 seconds. Strain into a 5-ounce martini glass.

SKINNY TIDBIT Sleek like a panther in a beautiful shade of pink, this SkinnyTini is versatile enough to be enjoyed with brunch or in place of a Cosmo on a ladies' night out.

POM-POM SKINNYTINI
135 CALORIES

2 ounces citrus vodka
1½ ounces diet ginger ale
1 ounce pomegranate juice
½ ounce light orange juice

Add all ingredients to a cocktail shaker with ice and shake for 10 to 15 seconds. Strain into a 5-ounce martini glass. Be careful as you shake any SkinnyTini containing a carbonated mixer, as it can have a powerful and slightly messy effect on your kitchen. To ease the situation, wrap the shaker in a towel and shake gently.

SKINNY TIDBIT The pomegranate martini was made famous by Oprah herself, and rightfully so! It's not just delicious; pomegranates are one of the most nutritious fruits you can eat. They are high in vitamin C and potassium, low in calories, and touted as a powerful antioxidant, helping protect you from cancer and heart disease.

PURE SUNSHINE
128 CALORIES

2 ounces citrus vodka
1½ ounces light lemonade
1 ounce light orange juice
½ ounce mango nectar
Orange wheel, for garnish

Add all ingredients except the orange wheel to a cocktail shaker with ice and shake for 10 to 15 seconds. Strain into a 5-ounce martini glass and float an orange wheel on top as a garnish to resemble the sun.

SKINNY TIDBIT Pure Sunshine, just as the name implies, is wonderfully bright and energizing. Be sure to chill the mixers and/or shake with ice extra-long to ensure it's ice-cold and refreshing and to reveal its cheerful, crisp taste.

THE SAMSONITE
150 CALORIES

2 ounces vanilla vodka
2 ounces nonfat milk
½ ounce light coconut milk
½ ounce sugar-free coconut syrup

Add all ingredients to a cocktail shaker with ice and shake for 10 to 15 seconds. Strain into a 5-ounce martini glass.

SKINNY TIDBIT To add a special flair to this cocktail, rim the glass with toasted coconut. To toast, sprinkle unsweetened shredded coconut on a baking sheet and bake at 350°F for 2 to 5 minutes. Check on it regularly and toss to avoid burning the edges. Simply sprinkle some on the top of the cocktail or rim the glass by dipping the edge of the martini glass in water and rolling the edges of the glass through the coconut before straining the martini from the shaker. Be sparing with the garnish; each teaspoon can easily add 12 to 20 additional calories.

SAUCY SENORITA
147 CALORIES

2 ounces white tequila
2 ounces light orange juice
½ ounce light ruby red grapefruit juice
½ ounce lime juice
10 drops liquid Sweet'N Low

Add all ingredients to a cocktail shaker with ice and shake for 10 to 15 seconds. Strain into a 5-ounce martini glass.

SKINNY TIDBIT Consider the Saucy Senorita to be a modern approach to the classic margarita. The white tequila pairs exquisitely with the sweet juices and sour citrus flavors. For the perfect touch, garnish the edges of the glass with rock salt and top off with a lime wedge. To rim the glass, dip the edges in water or lime juice and roll through a plate of rock salt to evenly cover the edges before straining the mixture from the shaker. The familiar salt rim adds zero extra calories, and the lime wedge less than 3!

THE SHAMROCK
136 CALORIES

2 ounces vodka
2 ounces Sugar-Free Red Bull
1 ounce Blue Gatorade

Add all ingredients to a cocktail shaker with ice and shake for 10 to 15 seconds. Strain into a 5-ounce martini glass. Be careful as you shake any SkinnyTini containing a carbonated mixer, as it can have a powerful and slightly messy effect on your kitchen. To ease the situation, wrap the shaker in a towel and shake gently.

SKINNY TIDBIT This drink is not the least bit Irish. It's named Shamrock for its brilliant green color. The mixture of Sugar-Free Red Bull and blue Gatorade is practically neon—a great SkinnyTini for the energy enthusiast!

SKINNY APPLETINI

133 CALORIES
ORIGINAL RECIPE: 287 CALORIES;
"SKINNY" RECIPE HAS 54 PERCENT FEWER CALORIES!

2 ounces apple vodka
3 ounces light apple juice

Add all ingredients to a cocktail shaker with ice and shake for 10 to 15 seconds. Strain into a 5-ounce martini glass.

SKINNY TIDBIT The appletini is one of the more popular martinis you'll see out in the bars. You'll find the Skinny Appletini more refreshing, as it lacks most of the strong sugary substances found in the common appletini. To make this simple and delicious SkinnyTini really special, make sure you garnish the glass with a sugar-cinnamon rim. Simply pour a small amount of apple juice on a plate and sprinkle 1 teaspoon of sugar and a dash of cinnamon on another plate. Dip the rim of the glass in the juice, then twist the glass in the sugar-cinnamon mix. This finishing touch will surprise and delight your guests, and only add 16 more calories. For the final flourish, garnish with a cinnamon stick!

SKINNY BELLINITINI

145 CALORIES
ORIGINAL RECIPE: 266 CALORIES;
"SKINNY" RECIPE HAS 46 PERCENT FEWER CALORIES!

1½ ounces vodka
2 ounces champagne
1 ounce light orange juice
½ ounce sugar-free peach syrup

Add all ingredients to a cocktail shaker with ice and shake for 10 to 15 seconds. Strain into a 5-ounce martini glass. Be careful as you shake any SkinnyTini containing a carbonated mixer, as it can have a powerful and slightly messy effect on your kitchen. To ease the situation, wrap the shaker in a towel and shake gently.

SKINNY TIDBIT
A standard BelliniTini contains peach schnapps, a very high-calorie alcohol that won't be missed when replaced with sugar-free peach-flavored syrup. The Skinny BelliniTini is a wonderful, light, summer afternoon cocktail to serve with lunch.

SKINNY SCREW
145 CALORIES

2 ounces vodka
2½ ounces light orange juice
½ ounce lemon juice

Add all ingredients to a cocktail shaker with ice and shake for 10 to 15 seconds. Strain into a 5-ounce martini glass.

SKINNY TIDBIT Like a traditional screwdriver with a sophisticated twist. Using fresh strained lemon juice will make it even more delicious, and fresh juice has almost twice the vitamin C as bottled. Also try replacing half the orange juice with diet ginger ale for a SkinnyTini that tastes as familiar as orange soda!

SKINNY CHOCOLATE MARTINI

148 CALORIES
ORIGINAL RECIPE: 453 CALORIES;
"SKINNY" RECIPE HAS 67 PERCENT FEWER CALORIES!

2 ounces strongly brewed coffee
2 ounces vanilla vodka
1 ounce low-fat milk (2%)
2 teaspoons fat-free hot cocoa mix

Be sure the coffee is cooled before adding it to the shaker with ice. Remember, hot liquids can have an explosive effect when shaken in an airtight container. Add all ingredients to a cocktail shaker with ice and shake for 10 to 15 seconds. Strain into a 5-ounce martini glass.

SKINNY TIDBIT A standard chocolate martini contains Irish cream, vodka, and chocolate liqueur, all of which come at a high caloric cost. In the Skinny version, the coffee mixed with hot cocoa provides a nice coffee-chocolate flavor, and the 2% milk gives it a rich consistency. You can use fat-free half-and-half for an even richer cocktail, with just 5 more calories. These clever replacements maintain the familiar flavors, and you'll only lose the calories! For a special touch with just 8 extra calories, drizzle 1 tablespoon of sugar-free chocolate syrup on the inside of the glass in a design of your choosing before you strain the martini into the glass.

SKINNY COSMOPOLITAN

129 CALORIES
ORIGINAL RECIPE: 287 CALORIES;
"SKINNY" RECIPE HAS 55 PERCENT FEWER CALORIES!

2 ounces citrus vodka
2½ ounces light cranberry juice
½ ounce light orange juice
¼ ounce (splash) lime juice

Add all ingredients to a cocktail shaker with ice and shake for 10 to 15 seconds. Strain into a 5-ounce martini glass.

SKINNY TIDBIT The original cosmo contains triple sec, an orange-flavored liqueur that has 80 calories per ounce and only 30 percent alcohol. Using natural fruit juice is a great way to eliminate unnecessary calories and still maintain the key flavors. If you prefer a more translucent cocktail, try sugar-free orange syrup instead of orange juice.

SKINNY LEMON DROP

136 CALORIES
ORIGINAL RECIPE: 212 CALORIES;
"SKINNY" RECIPE HAS 36 PERCENT FEWER CALORIES!

2 ounces vodka
2 ounces club soda
1 ounce lemon juice
10 drops liquid Sweet'N Low

Add all ingredients to a cocktail shaker with ice and shake for 10 to 15 seconds. Strain into a 5-ounce martini glass. Be careful as you shake any SkinnyTini containing a carbonated mixer, as it can have a powerful and slightly messy effect on your kitchen. To ease the situation, wrap the shaker in a towel and shake gently.

SKINNY TIDBIT
To enhance the elegance of this classic martini, be sure to rim the edges of the glass with fine sugar—a full teaspoon only adds 16 calories. To rim the glass, dip the edges in lemon juice and roll through a plate of superfine sugar to evenly cover the edges before straining the mixture from the shaker. It's easy to modify this cocktail for the true lemon enthusiast by simply adding more lemon juice or substituting light lemonade for the club soda.

SOPHIETINI
138 CALORIES

2 ounces premium vodka
1½ ounces club soda
1½ ounces lime-flavored water

Add all ingredients to a cocktail shaker with ice and shake for 10 to 15 seconds. Strain into a 5-ounce martini glass. Be careful as you shake any SkinnyTini containing a carbonated mixer, as it can have a powerful and slightly messy effect on your kitchen. To ease the situation, wrap the shaker in a towel and shake gently.

SKINNY TIDBIT The SophieTini, as the name implies, is sophisticated and fun. Its clear color and carbonation are accented beautifully by a garnish of fresh mint sprigs.

SPANISH MARTINI
126 CALORIES

1½ ounces vodka
1 ounce red wine
1 ounce diet ginger ale
1 ounce light orange juice
2 teaspoons lime juice
1 teaspoon sugar-free peach syrup

Add all ingredients to a cocktail shaker with ice and shake for 10 to 15 seconds. Be careful as you shake any SkinnyTini containing a carbonated mixer, as it can have a powerful and slightly messy effect on your kitchen. To ease the situation, wrap the shaker in a towel and shake gently. Strain into a 5-ounce martini glass.

SKINNY TIDBIT A creative twist on the traditional sangria. This low-calorie blend of vodka and wine may sound peculiar, but let the taste speak for itself. This SkinnyTini has it all: originality, flavor, distinction, and an ultralow calorie count. Be sure to garnish with an orange wedge to complete the look.

STRAWBERRY CHEESECAKE

151 CALORIES

2 ounces vanilla vodka
½ ounce sugar-free vanilla syrup
½ ounce fat-free vanilla coffee creamer
½ ounce lime juice
1 fresh strawberry
½ cup ice for blending

Add all ingredients including ice to a blender. Blend on high speed for a minute until mixture is liquid. Pour through a strainer into a martini glass to remove seeds and ice pieces and serve.

SKINNY TIDBIT The key to this unique SkinnyTini is to garnish it with a graham-cracker rim and a strawberry. The graham-cracker rim adds an extra 20 calories, the strawberry just 2. To prepare the martini glass, dip the rim in lime juice and then roll it in crushed graham crackers. The vanilla vodka, syrup, and creamer when combined with lime juice and fresh strawberry almost resembles the ever-familiar flavor of cheesecake. A great dessert cocktail if you're not in the mood for baking!

VANILLA CHAITINI
150 CALORIES

2 ounces strongly brewed vanilla chai tea
2 ounces vanilla vodka
1 ounce sugar-free coffee creamer

Be sure the tea is cooled before shaking. Remember, hot liquids can have an explosive effect when shaken in an airtight container. Add the tea and remaining ingredients to a cocktail shaker with ice and shake for 10 to 15 seconds. Strain into a 5-ounce martini glass.

SKINNY TIDBIT Chai tea is made by brewing tea with a mixture of aromatic spices. Chai simply means "tea" in India. You can find a recipe online for brewing your own chai, or you can opt for the much easier method of purchasing vanilla chai tea in the grocery store and steeping it in water. When you brew your tea, be sure to triple the recommended tea-to-water ratio to ensure it will carry enough flavor into the SkinnyTini.

SKINNY COCKTAIL RECIPES

REMINDER: Each Skinny Cocktail recipe contains 1.5 ounces of 80 proof alcohol (vodka, tequila, rum, or gin) and 3.5 ounces of low-calorie mixer and often have fewer than 120 calories.

CACTUS CHILL
130 CALORIES

1½ ounces tequila
¼ ounce agave nectar
½ ounce lime juice
2¾ ounces lime-flavored sparkling water

Pour the tequila, agave nectar, and lime juice into a highball or other cocktail glass and stir. Add ice and fill the glass with lime-flavored water.

SKINNY TIDBIT Agave has been used in Mexico as a natural sweetener for over a century and has very recently been making an impact in the United States as a replacement for high-fructose corn syrup. You can find it at most health food stores. While it is not a low-calorie sweetener, it is low on the glycemic index and 100 percent organic. Garnish this drink with a lime wedge.

DR. VANILLA VODKA
90 CALORIES

1½ ounces vanilla vodka
3½ ounces Diet Dr. Pepper

Pour all of the ingredients over ice into a highball or other cocktail glass.

SKINNY TIDBIT Surprisingly simple, yet surprisingly delicious! This is a great cocktail to serve when you have a large group over.

MEXICAN MOJITO
128 CALORIES

¼ ounce agave nectar
1 lime wedge
Fresh mint sprigs
1½ ounces white tequila
3½ ounces club soda

Add the agave nectar, lime wedge, and mint springs to a cocktail glass and muddle (mash up) the ingredients to bring out the flavors and pull the mint flavor into the liquid. Add ice and top with the tequila and club soda.

SKINNY TIDBIT Similar to the traditional mojito—with its refreshing combination of muddled mint, sweetener, and lime juice—but with white tequila and pure agave nectar instead of rum and sugar cane syrup, for a more southwestern flair. The Mexican Mojito is 100 percent natural and perfect to serve on a warm sunny afternoon, garnished with fresh mint.

SKINNY CAPE COD

113 CALORIES   ORIGINAL RECIPE: 149 CALORIES;
"SKINNY" RECIPE HAS 24 PERCENT FEWER CALORIES!

1½ ounces vodka
3½ ounces light cranberry juice

Pour all of the ingredients over ice into a highball or other cocktail glass.

SKINNY TIDBIT A fantastic and familiar cocktail also known as the Cape Codder. This simple recipe is the base for quite a few other highballs, including the sea breeze, the bay breeze, and the madras, to which other fruit flavors are added. All of them make great light, everyday drinks, especially on sunny, warm Saturday afternoons.

SKINNY BAY BREEZE

119 CALORIES ORIGINAL RECIPE: 151 CALORIES; "SKINNY" RECIPE HAS 21 PERCENT FEWER CALORIES!

1½ ounces vodka
3 ounces light cranberry juice
½ ounce pineapple juice

Pour all of the ingredients over ice into a highball or other cocktail glass.

SKINNY TIDBIT Some bay breeze recipes call for coconut rum or white rum instead of vodka, but the pineapple and the cranberry are consistent. If you go the rum route, stick to white rum. Coconut rum has 63 calories per ounce, but only half the alcohol potency, making it an inefficient use of alcohol calories.

SKINNY FUZZY NAVEL

115 CALORIES
ORIGINAL RECIPE: 261 CALORIES;
"SKINNY" RECIPE HAS 56 PERCENT FEWER CALORIES!

1½ ounce vodka
3 ounces light orange juice
½ ounce sugar-free peach syrup

Pour all of the ingredients over ice into a highball or other cocktail glass.

SKINNY TIDBIT The "fuzzy" in the name refers to the peach, and "navel" to the orange; all classic fuzzy navel recipes include these two key flavors. The Skinny Fuzzy Navel is one of the best examples of calorie efficiency. Your guests would never know you eliminated the schnapps and replaced it with sugar-free syrup, but they sure will thank you for saving them 56 percent of the calories!

SKINNY MADRAS

115 CALORIES
ORIGINAL RECIPE: 148 CALORIES;
"SKINNY" RECIPE HAS 22 PERCENT FEWER CALORIES!

1½ ounces vodka
2 ounces light cranberry juice
1½ ounces light orange juice

Pour all of the ingredients over ice into a highball or other cocktail glass.

SKINNY TIDBIT
The madras has delicious flavors; the full-calorie version can even be a simple substitute for a Cosmo when you're out with the ladies and trying to avoid downing all 300+ calories. To give a fresh look to this traditional cocktail, use blood-orange juice. It will add roughly 15 more calories, but the red pigment, anthocyanin, is an antioxidant that reduces risk for certain ailments, including age-related illnesses.

SKINNY LONG ISLAND ICED TEA

128 CALORIES
ORIGINAL RECIPE: 269 CALORIES; "SKINNY" RECIPE HAS 52 PERCENT FEWER CALORIES!

½ ounce vodka
½ ounce tequila
½ ounce rum
½ ounce gin
1½ ounces diet cola
1½ ounces diet lemon-lime soda

Pour all of the ingredients over ice into a highball or other cocktail glass.

SKINNY TIDBIT The original Long Island iced tea is high in calories, mostly thanks to the peculiarly high amounts of pure alcohol. A typical recipe will have roughly 4 ounces of 80 proof spirits!! While the Skinny version only has 2 ounces of alcohol (more than most cocktails), it will still give you the same flavors with less than half the calories.

SKINNY RUM PUNCH

129 CALORIES

ORIGINAL RECIPE: 219 CALORIES;
"SKINNY" RECIPE HAS 41 PERCENT FEWER CALORIES!

1 ounce white rum
2 ounces light orange juice
1 ounce pineapple juice
½ ounce lime juice
½ ounce dark rum

Add white rum and the juices to a highball or other cocktail glass with ice, then pour the dark rum on top and let it flow through the cocktail for a fun effect.

SKINNY TIDBIT Great for a Caribbean-themed party, served in a punch bowl. Go crazy with fresh fruit garnishes to give it even more flair. Try making fresh fruit kabobs by skewering limes, orange slices, maraschino cherries, and pineapple for your guests to drop in their drinks and snack on throughout the evening.

SKINNY MARGARITA

138 CALORIES

ORIGINAL RECIPE: 303 CALORIES;
"SKINNY" RECIPE HAS 54 PERCENT FEWER CALORIES!

1½ ounces tequila
1½ ounces light orange juice
1½ ounces grapefruit juice
½ ounce lime juice
10 drops liquid Sweet'N Low

Pour all of the ingredients over ice into a highball or other cocktail glass.

SKINNY TIDBIT
The traditional margarita, while certainly a long-time favorite, is unfortunately loaded with calories from the sweet-and-sour mix and the triple sec. Balancing fresh citrus juices with sweetener is a great way to eliminate the empty calories and maintain the sugary-tart flavors you expect from a margarita.

SKINNY MOJITO

96 CALORIES
ORIGINAL RECIPE: 140 CALORIES;
"SKINNY" RECIPE HAS 31 PERCENT FEWER CALORIES!

15 drops liquid Sweet'N Low
Lime wedge
Fresh mint sprigs
1½ ounces white rum
3½ ounces club soda

Add the sweetener, lime, and mint springs to a highball or other cocktail glass and muddle (mash up) the ingredients to pull out the flavors. Add ice and top with rum and club soda.

SKINNY TIDBIT The mojito originated in Havana and quickly become a hit in the United States, thanks to the fresh flavors of mint and lime muddled with sugar. Replacing the sugar with sweetener is easy and gives you a Skinny Cocktail that is refreshing, hip, and ultralow in calories. For a classic look, be sure to garnish with additional fresh mint.

SKINNY MUDSLIDE

134 CALORIES
ORIGINAL RECIPE: 443 CALORIES;
"SKINNY" RECIPE HAS 70 PERCENT FEWER CALORIES!

1 ounce strongly brewed coffee
1½ ounces vanilla vodka
1 ounce sugar-free vanilla coffee creamer
2 tsp fat-free hot cocoa mix
½–1 cup ice

Pour all ingredients into a blender. Be sure the coffee is cooled before blending so that it does not melt the ice. This will give you a fairly liquid cocktail; use more ice and a tad bit more coffee if you want to froth up the drink. Mix on high speed for a minute, pour into a cocktail glass or beer mug, and serve.

SKINNY TIDBIT DELICIOUS! It may be hard to imagine a Mudslide that's low on calories, but wait till you try this. Eliminating the Irish cream, Kahlua, and ice cream and replacing them with the clever Skinny ingredients produces a cocktail that is sure to surprise and delight your friends.

SKINNY PIÑA COLADA

124 CALORIES
ORIGINAL RECIPE: 242 CALORIES;
"SKINNY" RECIPE HAS 49 PERCENT FEWER CALORIES!

1½ ounces white rum
1 ounce light coconut milk
½ ounce pineapple juice
½ ounce sugar-free coconut syrup
½–1 cup ice

Pour all ingredients including the ice into a blender. This will give you a fairly liquid cocktail; use more ice (you may need to add just a tiny bit of water as well) if you want to froth up the drink. Mix on high speed for a minute; pour into a cocktail or hurricane glass, and serve.

SKINNY TIDBIT
This surprising treat is both a blessing and a curse—it is truly better than the original piña colada, making it far too easy to overindulge! Be sure to garnish with the traditional pineapple wedge and maraschino cherry to give it a classic look and feel.

SKINNY SANGRIA

115 CALORIES
ORIGINAL RECIPE: 188 CALORIES;
"SKINNY" RECIPE HAS 39 PERCENT FEWER CALORIES!

2 ounces red wine
1 ounce white rum
1½ ounces light orange juice
½ ounce light ruby red grapefruit juice
20 drops liquid Sweet'N Low
Dash of cinnamon

Add all ingredients to a cocktail shaker with ice and shake for 5 to 10 seconds. Pour into a wine glass over ice.

SKINNY TIDBIT The ruby red grapefruit juice and cinnamon put a delicious twist on the traditional sangria. The bulk of the calorie savings are won by replacing the pure sugar with sweetener. For a special touch, try garnishing with orange slices.

SKINNY SEX ON THE BEACH

118 CALORIES
ORIGINAL RECIPE: 168 CALORIES;
"SKINNY" RECIPE HAS 30 PERCENT FEWER CALORIES!

1½ ounces vodka
1½ ounces light cranberry juice
1 ounce light orange juice
½ ounce pineapple juice
½ ounce sugar-free peach syrup

Pour all of the ingredients over ice into a highball or other cocktail glass.

SKINNY TIDBIT This fun and fruity cocktail was originally made popular by a notable restaurant chain. The bulk of the calorie savings in this Skinny version comes from replacing peach schnapps with sugar-free peach syrup, which maintains the sweet citrus flavor that's sure to please any drink enthusiast.

SKINNY STRAWBERRY DAIQUIRI

110 CALORIES ORIGINAL RECIPE: 366 CALORIES; "SKINNY" RECIPE HAS 70 PERCENT FEWER CALORIES!

1½ ounces white rum
1½ ounces sugar-free strawberry-flavored water
½ ounce lime juice
5 strawberries
5 drops liquid Sweet'N Low
½ cup ice for blending

Pour all ingredients into a blender. This will give you a fairly liquid cocktail; use more ice and a tad bit more strawberry water if you want to froth up the drink. Mix on high speed for a minute, pour into a glass, and serve.

SKINNY TIDBIT Top off this delicious fresh fruit cocktail with more fresh strawberries and fat-free whipped topping for a truly decadent experience.

SKINNY TEQUILA SUNSET

133 CALORIES
ORIGINAL RECIPE: 208 CALORIES;
"SKINNY" RECIPE HAS 36 PERCENT FEWER CALORIES!

1½ ounces tequila
2 ounces light orange juice
1 ounce lemon juice
½ ounce grapefruit juice
4 drops liquid Sweet'N Low
Splash of grenadine

Add the tequila, juices, and sweetener to a highball or other cocktail glass with ice, then pour the grenadine on top and let it flow through the cocktail for a fun effect.

SKINNY TIDBIT
A tangy twist on the margarita. Enjoy this cocktail in the afternoon summer sunshine, garnished with lemon wedges. The bulk of the calorie savings in this recipe comes from replacing the honey, which has 128 calories per ounce! The Tequila Sunset complements the margarita well for a Mexican-themed party.

SKINNY TOM COLLINS

104 CALORIES
ORIGINAL RECIPE: 147 CALORIES;
"SKINNY" RECIPE HAS 29 PERCENT FEWER CALORIES!

1½ ounces gin
2½ ounces club soda
1 ounce fresh lemon juice
10 drops liquid Sweet'N Low

Pour all of the ingredients over ice into a highball or other cocktail glass.

SKINNY TIDBIT
The original Tom Collins recipe calls for a teaspoon of pure sugar. Simply replacing that with liquid Sweet'N Low could save a moderate drinker who consumes one to two drinks 34 calories per day. Knowing that daily 3,500 excess calories equals 1 pound of weight, tally that up over the course of a year and it's over 3 pounds! This is a great example of how the smallest changes can really add up in the end. Be sure to garnish with a lemon wedge.

SWEET TART
116 CALORIES

1½ ounces vodka
2½ ounces light cranberry juice
½ ounce lemon juice
½ ounce lime juice
10 drops liquid Sweet'N Low

Pour all of the ingredients over ice into a highball or other cocktail glass.

SKINNY TIDBIT This adorable pink cocktail is just as tasty and tangy as its namesake. Strong citrus from the lemon and lime juices is eased with the liquid sweetener. For an extra-fresh flavor, be sure to use fresh lemon and lime juices.

VANILLA SIPPER
90 CALORIES

1½ ounces vanilla vodka
3½ ounces diet ginger ale

Pour all of the ingredients over ice into a highball or other cocktail glass.

SKINNY TIDBIT This sweet, vanilla-flavored cocktail is delicious. It has 31 percent fewer calories than a similar drink made with full-calorie ginger ale.

LOVE THE RECIPES... BUT WHAT DO I DO WHEN I'M OUT?

You can get as creative and as clever as you want with all the low-sugar and sugar-free mixers that are on the grocery store shelves today. But that won't be all that useful when you find yourself at a local bar trying to order up a Skinny AppleTini or Cosmo for yourself. Not to fear! You can still go out for the night with your girlfriends and make smart decisions. Use the following recipes, which you should be able to order almost anywhere and at a very reasonable calorie "cost." These recipes are broken into two categories: "Easy Peasy" and "Entails Just a Little Creativity." Easy Peasy, as the name implies, includes readily available cocktails you can just order from the bartender with little effort. Entails Just a Little Creativity is a fun section, perfect for the SkinnyTini drinker who likes to use her witty charm to get the bartender to make the exact cocktail she wants.

EASY PEASY

BEER AND WINE

5-ounce White Wine Spritzer: 55 Calories A wine spritzer is simply 50 percent white wine and 50 percent soda water, cutting the calories exactly in half. Order it that way directly from the server, or split a glass of white wine and a soda water in a wine glass with a girlfriend and save 50 percent of the cost!

12-ounce Nonalcoholic Beer: 60 Calories Nonalcoholic beer, while not an alcoholic cocktail, is included in this section because of the significant calorie savings. Depending on your social objectives, this can be a very good option.

5-ounce Glass of Champagne: 100 Calories Champagne is a great Skinny Girl drink. It's available almost anywhere, fairly low in calories, and extremely elegant and classy!

12-ounce Light Beer: 100 Calories Light beers vary in total calories depending on the brand and the relative alcohol potency. You can find ultralight versions that have as few as 60 calories per serving, but be prepared for half the alcohol potency as well.

5-ounce Glass of Wine: 110 Calories An average 5-ounce serving of most wines will contain around 100 to 120 calories. The actual number of calories will vary, depending on the total alcohol potency and sugar content, which is contingent on the grape variety, climate, vintage, and style.

12-ounce Guinness: 128 Calories Guinness is surprisingly low in calories for its rich, hearty flavors. Another great thing about stout beers is that you can drink them slowly, as they do not have to be served chilled. Careful with the alcohol potency—if you order an "extra stout" version at 6 percent, you'll also have 40 percent more calories.

BLOODY MARY
116 CALORIES

1½ ounces vodka
3½ ounces tomato juice
1 dash lemon juice
½ teaspoon Worcestershire sauce
2 drops Tabasco sauce

Pour all of the ingredients over ice into a highball or other cocktail glass.

SKINNY TIDBIT Celery salt is a fantastic seasoning agent that brings much more than just a salty flavor. Its unique, savory taste flatters the other ingredients of the Bloody Mary beautifully. Ask the bartender to include it for a distinctive, delicious flavor and zero extra calories! Be sure your Bloody Mary is topped off a with lime wedge and celery stick garnish.

GREYHOUND
135 CALORIES

1½ ounces vodka
3½ ounces grapefruit juice

Pour all of the ingredients over ice into a highball or other cocktail glass.

SKINNY TIDBIT Grapefruit juice is a great Skinny ingredient. It is stocked in most bars, is high in vitamin C, and comes with only 11 calories per ounce.

MIMOSA
92 CALORIES

2 ounces orange juice
3 ounces champagne

Add the orange juice to a champagne flute and top with the champagne.

SKINNY TIDBIT Add to the elegance of a traditional mimosa by garnishing with fresh fruit. Try strawberries, peaches, or even blueberries to bring extra nutrition and color to your mimosa! If enjoying your drink at home, you can save an additional 20 calories by using light orange juice and make it a Skinny Mimosa.

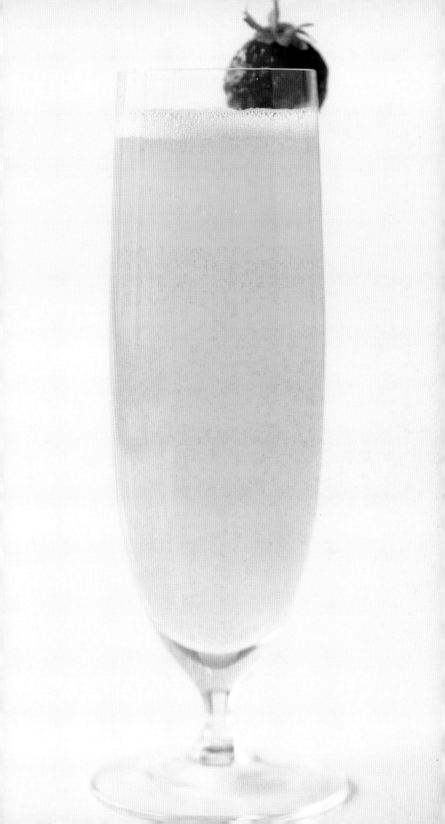

IRISH COFFEE
99 CALORIES

1½ ounces Irish whisky
3½ ounces hot coffee
1 packet of sugar-free sweetener

Pour all of the ingredients into a cocktail glass and stir to dissolve the sweetener.

SKINNY TIDBIT You can have the bartender add skim milk for just an additional 10 calories per ounce if you prefer a lighter look and flavor.

LIQUOR WITH DIET SODA
(A.K.A. SKINNY BITCH)
96 CALORIES

1½ ounces vodka or other liquor
3½ ounces diet soda

Pour all of the ingredients over ice into a highball or other cocktail glass.

SKINNY TIDBIT This very generic combination of liquor and diet soda is becoming known as a Skinny Bitch across the country. Whisky and Coke, rum and Coke, and vodka and 7-Up can be delicious flavor combinations! Regular soda has roughly 13 calories per ounce, so it's easy to save nearly 50 calories per drink with diet soda If you consume one drink per day, this would save you over 18,000 calories over the course of a year. That's over 5 pounds of weight! Garnish with a lemon or lime wedge.

SKINNY CUBA LIBRE
103 CALORIES

1½ ounces dark rum
3 ounces diet cola
½ ounce lime juice
Lime wedge

Pour all of the ingredients except the lime wedge over ice into a high-ball or other cocktail glass. Garnish with the lime wedge.

SKINNY TIDBIT Essentially a rum and Coke with a little lime. Ordering a Cuba Libre may ensure it is served with name-brand rum and cost you a few extra bucks. If you don't mind well rum, simply ask for rum and Diet Coke with lime.

SEA BREEZE
143 CALORIES

1½ ounces vodka
2 ounces cranberry juice
1½ ounce grapefruit juice

Pour all of the ingredients over ice into a highball or other cocktail glass.

SKINNY TIDBIT If you opt to make this drink at home, you can substitute light ruby red grapefruit juice for the regular grapefruit juice and light cranberry juice in this recipe. It will provide a sweeter taste and save more calories, bringing the total count down to just 113.

"SKINNY" RED BULL WITH VODKA
100 CALORIES

1½ ounces vodka
3½ ounces Sugar-Free Red Bull

Pour all of the ingredients over ice into a highball or other cocktail glass.

SKINNY TIDBIT An entire 8.5-ounce can of Sugar-Free Red Bull has just 10 calories, making it a fantastic Skinny mixer that many bars and restaurants are currently serving. All you have to do is dance for 13 minutes to burn off the entire cocktail!

VODKA SODA
96 CALORIES

1½ ounces vodka
3½ ounces club soda

Pour the vodka and club soda into a highball or other cocktail glass.

SKINNY TIDBIT You can dress this cocktail up by trying any of the flavored vodkas available or by garnishing it with a lime wedge. Raspberry vodka with extra limes is a delicious and very easy to order option!

VODKA TONIC
131 CALORIES

1½ ounces vodka
3½ ounces tonic water

Pour the vodka and tonic over ice into a highball or other cocktail glass.

SKINNY TIDBIT Vodka tonic: the most classic cocktail of all. Many confuse tonic water with club soda, which can be a calorically expensive mistake, as tonic has nearly as many calories as regular soda. But in comparison to most popular cocktails, this is still a good option. If you are making one at home, diet tonic water can be found in most grocery stores by scouring the alcohol mix section carefully and can save you 27 percent of the calories. Garnish with a lime wedge.

ENTAILS JUST A LITTLE CREATIVITY

BERRY BLISS
136 CALORIES

1½ ounces vodka
3½ ounces club soda
½ ounce (splash) crème de cassis

Pour all of the ingredients over ice into a highball or other cocktail glass.

SKINNY TIDBIT Crème de cassis is a blood-red, sweet, black currant–flavored liqueur that is very popular in France. It is often mixed with champagne, but is also a great addition to a traditional vodka soda. Its rich color and delightful flavor are sure to add variety and but a few calories to your social routine!

BLACK VELVET
80 CALORIES

2½ ounces Guinness
2½ ounces champagne

Fill a champagne flute halfway with Guinness and top off with champagne. To achieve the best effect, pour over an upside-down spoon so the liquid runs down the sides of the glass slowly. This prevents the beer and the champagne from splashing into each other and allows the different densities to remain largely in separate layers.

SKINNY TIDBIT Sounds peculiar, but may be worth trying if you are one who likes both champagne and stout. The flavor combinations are intriguing, to say the least!

CRANBERRY BUBBLY
101 CALORIES

1½ ounces cranberry vodka
3 ounces club soda
½ ounce (splash) cranberry juice

Pour all of the ingredients over ice into a highball or other cocktail glass.

SKINNY TIDBIT Similar to the Fruit Basket. You can easily personalize this recipe with your favorite flavors by simply ordering your preferred flavored vodka with club soda and asking the bartender to include a splash of the corresponding juice. Garnish with a lime wedge.

GINGERBERRY
141 CALORIES

1½ ounces vodka
2½ ounces ginger ale
1 ounce cranberry juice

Pour all of the ingredients over ice into a highball or other cocktail glass.

SKINNY TIDBIT Gingerberry is refreshing and has a great bite! Be sure to ask the bartender for real ginger ale. Sometimes a bartender will mix clear and dark sodas together. It's easier for the bar, but unfortunately, the flavor suffers.

MELON FIZZ
136 CALORIES

1½ ounces vodka
1½ ounces club soda
½ ounce (splash) Midori

Pour all of the ingredients over ice into a highball or other cocktail glass.

SKINNY TIDBIT Midori is the beautiful green liqueur with the refreshing and fruity taste of melon. It is high in calories if enjoyed in large doses, but when you mix it with club soda, you can cut the calories and still get the vibrant melon flavor.

SKINNY LEMONADE
88 CALORIES

1½ ounces citrus vodka
3 ounces club soda
½ ounce lemon juice
1 packet of sugar-free sweetener

Pour all of the ingredients over ice into a highball or other cocktail glass. Stir to dissolve the sweetener.

SKINNY TIDBIT Similar to a lemon drop, minus the strong alcohol content and potent lemon taste. When ordering, simply ask for a citron or citrus vodka and soda, with extra lemon, and snag a sweetener packet off one of the tables. If you're making this drink at home, use liquid Sweet'N Low—it will dissolve into the cocktail better.

SKINNY MAI TAI
148 CALORIES

2½ ounces orange juice
1 ounce pineapple juice
1 ounce (splash) white rum

Pour all of the ingredients over ice into a highball or other cocktail glass.

SKINNY TIDBIT To simplify ordering this cocktail, request white rum with orange juice with a splash of pineapple juice and dark rum. The calories may not be exact, but the bartender will be less likely to be annoyed.

STRAWBERRY SPLASH
132 CALORIES

1½ ounces vodka
3 ounces club soda
½ ounce (splash) strawberry schnapps

Pour all of the ingredients over ice into a highball or other cocktail glass.

SKINNY TIDBIT Enjoy this cocktail while you are out and craving a strawberry daiquiri but don't want to indulge in the 380 calories. The strawberry schnapps provides a sweet, fruity flavor and the club soda provides a refreshing bite!

RASPBERRY LEMONADE
101 CALORIES

1½ ounces vodka
3½ ounces club soda
½ packet sugar-free raspberry lemonade powder

Pour all of the ingredients over ice into a highball or other cocktail glass. Stir to dissolve the powder.

SKINNY TIDBIT This is a very clever SkinnyTini, because the packet of sugar-free flavored powder has to be brought to the bar in your purse or pocket! Simply purchase a box from the water aisle at the grocery store, and drop a few packets in your purse. Order a vodka soda, and add roughly half the packet to the cocktail. You will have a delightful colored and flavored cocktail for minimal extra calories!

WINE COCKTAIL
89 CALORIES

3 ounces white wine
1 ounce orange juice
1 ounce cranberry juice

Pour the wine into a white wine glass and top off with the juices. It's okay to add ice to keep the drink cool.

SKINNY TIDBIT Similar to a mimosa, with an unfamiliar but likable flavor and color! This is a wonderful cocktail to order at brunch with your girl-friends, as it is delicious, pink, and ultralow in calories!

THE SKINNY
TRICKS

KNOW YOUR GARNISHES

It's easy to forget all the fun little treats that come skewered in our fancy cocktails or that are hidden under the ever-so-cute paper umbrellas. But those extras, while very tiny, can really add up! It's almost frightening to see that two tablespoons of full-fat whipped cream can add 50 calories to your favorite cocktail! On the positive side, there are many garnishes that add flavor, aesthetic appeal, and very few calories. Familiarize yourself with the information in the table below. Take note of the items, and don't forget that the calories in these garnishes, even though they may just be there for looks, count if you eat them!

GARNISH	SERVING SIZE	CALORIES
Cinnamon stick	1 stick	0
Cocktail onion	1 onion	0
Lemon twist	1 twist	0
Mint leaves	2 leaves	0
Celery stick	1 stick	0
Strawberry	1 strawberry	0
Lemon wedge	⅛ lemon	2
Lime wedge	⅛ lime	3
Orange wheel	1/10 orange	7
Pineapple wedge	¼ slice, ½" thick	7
Maraschino cherry	1 cherry	8
Olive	2 olives	8
Pimiento-stuffed olive	2 olives	8
Sugar-free chocolate syrup	1 Tbsp	8
Toasted coconut	1 Tbsp	15
Fat-free whipped topping	2 Tbsp	15
Sugar-cinnamon rim	1 Tsp	16
Cocoa-powdered rim (unsweetened)	1 Tsp	19
Graham cracker crumbs	1 Tbsp	20
Blue cheese–stuffed olive	2 olives	20
Shaved chocolate	1 Tsp	25
Cocoa-powder rim (sweetened)	1 Tsp	44
Whipped cream	2 Tbsp	52

MANAGING YOUR WEIGHT AND SOCIAL LIFE

In addition to learning to make lower-calorie choices when preparing and ordering cocktails, you can also practice a few simple behavior modifications to better manage your weight while still enjoying your social life.

The single most important thing to remember when drinking alcohol is MODERATION! What is moderation? Well, the U.S. Department of Agriculture and the Dietary Guidelines for Americans recommend not exceeding two drinks per day if you are a man or one drink per day if you are a woman. If you're anything like me, your next question is "Can I save up all my moderate daily cocktails for one Friday night?" Unfortunately, several articles have been published that don't support that strategy. Moderation should clearly occur in small doses over time, not in large doses all at once.

SAVE CALORIES AND CASH: PACE YOURSELF WITHOUT BEING A PARTY POOPER

This tip is not rocket science by any means, but when you put it into practice, it may be just as helpful! The concept is to select a cocktail that can be easily ordered without alcohol. You order yourself a normal cocktail, and then rotate every other with a virgin version. This is also known as the cocktail/mocktail trick. Vodka soda with lime is a perfect example. You order one standard, and then you order just a club soda with lime. Remember to ask the bartender to serve it in a standard cocktail glass, not a water glass, to avoid blowing your cover.

The perks of this technique are plentiful! First, you save 96 calories and roughly five dollars each time you order the virgin version. Second, you don't spoil anybody's night out by saying "I'm not drinking tonight," thereby making everybody else feel guilty for indulging themselves. The last and potentially best perk of this technique: no hangover! It's virtually impossible to get wasted or wake up hung-over if you've paced yourself properly. This allows you to be productive the following day, and to burn more calories through activity! The next section will show you how long you need to partake in daily sporty, relaxing, or fun activities to do just that.

Next time you're out drinking, remember how much more fun it is to go play catch in the park, go kayaking on a lake, or even walk around a shopping mall on a Sunday afternoon than to lie in bed feeling like you are going to die. Use that motivation to order a mocktail or a virgin drink!

EARN YOUR PARTY!
MINDLESS, CREATIVE, AND HILARIOUS WAYS TO BURN CALORIES

We talk about "burning calories through activity," and understandably, that doesn't sound like fun to the vast majority of the population. Some of us have conditioned ourselves to dread activity and consider it some form of punishment for over-indulging elsewhere. But keep in mind that activity does not have to be painful, and you don't need to be in a gym to burn calories.

This section lists more than sixty activities and the number of minutes you need to engage in each activity to burn an average of 100 calories. Obviously, actual numbers will vary, but the point is to give you a general idea how these different activities can help you balance your caloric equation. If you want to con-

RELAXING ACTIVITIES

ACTIVITY	MINUTES REQUIRED TO BURN 100 CALORIES	
	130 lbs	180 lbs
Bikram yoga	10	7
Hatha yoga	26	19
Tai chi	26	19
Stretching	26	19
Pilates	29	21

DAILY ROUTINE ACTIVITIES

ACTIVITY	MINUTES REQUIRED TO BURN 100 CALORIES	
	130 lbs	180 lbs
Mowing lawn	19	13
Gardening	20	15
Vacuuming	23	16
Playing with kids	26	19
General cleaning	31	21

sume more calories through cocktails, but still fit into your favorite pair of skinny jeans, you'd better be prepared to burn those calories. And don't ever underestimate the calories you burn doing everyday activities. Believe it or not, you may actually have earned a reward for your rigorous cleaning efforts!

PHYSICAL EXERCISE ACTIVITIES — MINUTES REQUIRED TO BURN 100 CALORIES

ACTIVITY	130 lbs	180 lbs
Running up stairs	7	5
Running, 7½ mph	8	6
Running uphill	9	7
Running, 6 mph	10	7
Swimming laps	13	9
Jogging, 5 mph	13	9
Biking, moderate	15	11
Aerobics	15	12
Weight lifting, vigorous	17	12
Stair stepper	17	12
Walking, 3 mph	29	21
Weight lifting, moderate	34	25
Strolling, 2 mph	41	29

SPORTY ACTIVITIES — MINUTES REQUIRED TO BURN 100 CALORIES

ACTIVITY	130 lbs	180 lbs
Boxing, ring	8	6
Karate	10	7
Rowing	11	8
Jumping jacks	13	9
Tennis, singles	13	9
Basketball	13	9
Soccer	15	11
Boxing, punching bag	17	12
Tennis, doubles	17	12
Golf, carrying clubs	19	13
Push-ups	23	16
Driving range	34	25

FUN ACTIVITIES

ACTIVITY	130 lbs	180 lbs
Rock climbing	9	7
Touch football	13	9
Scuba diving	15	11
Roller skating	15	11
Ice skating	15	11
Horseback riding	16	11
Cross-country hiking	17	12
Waterskiing	17	12
Snow skiing	13	12
Dancing	19	13
Kayaking	20	15
Ping Pong	26	19
Fishing	26	19
Surfing	34	25
Frisbee	34	25
Miniature golf	34	25
Bowling	34	25
Pool (billiards)	41	29
Croquet	41	29
Wall or lawn darts	41	29
Catch	41	29

Calculations were done for 130- and 180-pound individuals. You will see a significant difference between the two weights when considering the amount of time required to burn 100 calories. This is because larger people tend to have more muscle mass. Muscle is simply more expensive to maintain, and hence burns calories more quickly.

Look at the charts above and play with the numbers. It is interesting to toy with them and work out balancing equations for each exercise. Sample equations may help you decide whether or not the cocktail is worth the physical effort required to burn off the calories.

Think of burning calories as a balancing act to even out your cocktail consumption. Look at it as a see-saw. If you are going to weigh down one end with 300 extra calories from two SkinnyTinis, what activity will you add to even it out? Will it be 93 minutes of cleaning your house, 51 minutes of waterskiing, or 30 minutes of running? After you select your favorite SkinnyTinis, review the charts and do the math to figure out how long you'll need to engage in your favorite activities. Below are sample balancing acts to help get you started.

- Is it worth a 30-minute stroll after brunch with your friends to work off the mimosa you enjoyed?

- Is it worth cleaning our own house before a dinner party for 20 to 30 minutes so you can enjoy a guilt-free glass of wine?

- Would you enjoy hitting the driving range for an hour a week to burn an additional 240 calories, then indulging in two light beers at the club house?

- When at a bar, why not play pool or Ping-Pong to burn off your alcohol calories instead of sitting on a stool?

- How about adding a 30-minute yoga or tai chi lesson to your week and enjoying a guilt-free Skinny Chocolate Martini after a long day in the office?

- Dancing is always a good idea—just 20 minutes per 100-calorie cocktail!

- If you're looking for a fun way to spend an evening, try miniature golfing. Burn over 200 calories and enjoy up to two SkinnyTinis!

KNOW YOUR LIMITS
PACE YOURSELF SO YOU AREN'T THE PARTY POOPER

Another good tactic when balancing your alcohol consumption is to simply know when enough is enough. The worst thing you can do to your body, your reputation, and your friends is to drink too much, make an ass of yourself, get into some sort of fight, and end up barfing in the toilet (if you're lucky) at the end of the night. Nobody likes a messy drunk. The following strategies will show you how to avoid being "That Girl."

SKINNY GIRL'S DRINKING TIPS AND TRICKS

- Know your limit and don't exceed it. Most people find that they can consume one drink per hour without any ill effects. Experiment with this number and stay on track while you are out and about.

- Move around! Don't sit on a stool and drink. Use the charts on pages 136 to 138 to see how long it takes for each activity to burn 100 calories. Burn up those alcohol calories so they don't turn into fat!

- Practice the Saving Calories and Cash technique. This technique is discussed in detail on page 135 and offers multiple benefits, including pacing your alcohol absorption.

- Know what you're drinking. Some cocktails have so many ingredients you just don't know how many calories or how much alcohol you are consuming. This can catch you off guard and prompt you to overconsume. Use the charts on pages 8 and 9 to become a smart, skinny social drinker!

- Eat while you drink. Food will help slow the absorption of alcohol into your body. And who doesn't love a little snack along with a cocktail anyway? Be sure to account for the extra calories in your daily balancing act.

- Make a plan. Be proactive and decide before you go out how much you want to drink, how much money you want to spend, and how much you want to move around while you are out. Tell your friends so they can help you stick to it.

- Drink slowly. There is no rush when it comes to finishing cocktails. Drinking faster will just cost you more money and calories. Take time to enjoy and savor the quality of the liquor you are consuming. Shots are not a part of the Skinny Girl's plan!

- Drink water. Alcohol is known to be dehydrating. Dehydration triggers thirst, which in turn can prompt you to drink more alcohol. Sneaking in a glass of water between drinks will help stave off dehydration and the biological urge to consume more.

- If you're not up for drinking, don't drink. If you're facing peer pressure, or you just don't want to be rude, simply accept a drink and replace it with a nonalcoholic version without the host knowing. Or you can accidentally "lose" it by setting it down and walking away. Your host will likely be too distracted to even notice.

- Set your drink down. Between sips, give your wrist a rest or engage in some other activity. Keeping your hands off your cocktail can significantly delay consumption.

CONCLUSION

We can enjoy cocktails and their positive effects on our lives. We don't have to give up the little treats that help make life worth living. AND we don't have to be alcoholics, gluttons, or gain weight when we do drink! As with everything, it is all about moderation and balancing the calories you consume with the calories you burn. A little creativity and ingenuity helps along the way when trying to finagle your favorite cocktail into your routine. Cheers to that!

INDEX